P9-DMD-503

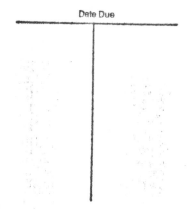

SPORTS CAR RACING

by Matt Doeden

Jan Lahtonen, consultant, safety engineer, and auto mechanic

Lerner Publications Company • Minneapolis

For Dad

Cover Photo: Driver Nick Ham, in his Mazda RX-8 (#70), leads a group of GT cars during the 2007 Rolex 24 in Miami, Florida.

Lerner Publications Company
A division of Lerner Publishing Group, Inc.
241 First Avenue North
Minneapolis, MN 55401 U.S.A.

Website address: www.lernerbooks.com

Library of Congress Cataloging-in-Publication Data

Doeden, Matt.
      Sports car racing / by Matt Doeden.
          p.   cm. — (Motor mania)
      Includes bibliographical references and index.
      ISBN 978–0–8225–9429–1 (lib. bdg. : alk. paper)
      1. Sports car racing—Juvenile literature.
   2. Grand Prix racing—Juvenile literature. I. Title.
   GV1029.D64   2009
   796.72—dc22   2008025573

Manufactured in the United States of America
1 2 3 4 5 6 – DP – 14 13 12 11 10 09

Contents

Introduction

Sports cars are built for speed and performance. They're made for zooming down the road and taking turns at top speed. So it's only natural that so many fans love the thrill of sports car racing. Fans love to smell the burning rubber and hear the engines roar as the world's fastest sports cars are pushed to their limits.

Sports car racing has been around almost since the dawn of the automobile. Early races like the Le Mans 24 Hours shaped the sport. Sports car racing focuses on the performance of the car more than the driver. From short sprints to long endurance races, the sport has plenty of excitement and variety. And it has a loyal following. It may not rival the popularity of stock car racing or open-wheel racing. But for sports car fans, nothing beats seeing a sleek Audi or Porsche tame the toughest track.

Fans on the hillside watch
a pair of passing sports cars
during a race in Ohio in 2007.

Chapter One

SPORTS CAR RACING HISTORY

Below: Spectators line the track as cars race down a straightaway in the 1928 Le Mans 24 Hours.

It was May 26, 1923. Dozens of cars were lining up in rows of two just outside the town of Le Mans, France. A cold rain fell on those gathered there that day. But the rain didn't dampen the excitement of the drivers and fans awaiting the start of a new 24-hour race. Nobody knew it at the time, but this was the beginning of a new era of car racing.

Modern sports car racing can trace its roots back to this day. The earliest sports cars, with model names like the Bentley Sport and the Bignan Desmo, looked nothing like modern sports cars. But they would blaze the trail that made sports car racing such a popular sport worldwide.

The Le Mans 24 Hours was a brand-new idea. It wasn't about pure speed, like the popular Grand Prix races of the time. Cars didn't complete a set number of laps and cross a finish line to win. Instead, the endurance race was designed to push a car to its limits by running it day and night, for 24 hours straight.

Cars drove on a circuit, or course, of more than 10 miles (16 kilometers) on the roads surrounding the town. The car that covered the most distance (made the most circuits) was the winner. The race was so demanding that one driver wasn't enough. Each car had a team of two drivers who took turns behind the wheel.

Originally, the competition was to take place over three races and three

A Bentley sports car passes a crashed Lagonda as it rounds a turn during the 1928 Le Mans. This Bentley, driven by Henry Birkin and Jean Chassagne, came in fifth place in the race, while another Bentley took first prize.

Building a Legend

The winners of the first Le Mans 24 were André Lagache and René Léonard. They drove a Chenard & Walcker Sport and completed 1,373 miles (2,210 km) during the race. Their average speed was about 57 miles (92 km) per hour. But almost as famously, a Bentley in the race soldiered on through the night despite a broken headlight and a damaged fuel tank. The never-say-die effort of the Bentley's drivers helped fuel the popularity of the young sport.

A Bentley sports car during the 1923 Le Mans 24 Hours

years. The winner would be awarded a prize called the Rudge-Whitworth Triennial Cup. But before long, race organizers realized that having a champion every year was a better idea.

Growth of the Sport

After that first race, the Le Mans 24 exploded in popularity. Teams from around Europe competed. Over the next decade, the Bentley was the dominant car. By the 1930s, automakers were beginning to alter car designs to better suit racing. Models like the Alfa Romeo and the Bugatti became more aerodynamic, shaped to cut through the air with little resistance. This allowed them to pick up more speed on the course's straight sections. Their success in racing translated to sales for the manufacturers.

The sideshow surrounding the race was also taking shape. Race organizers knew most people would get bored during a 24-hour event. So they created a circuslike atmosphere around the race. Fireworks displays, music, and dancing were just a few of the distractions offered. The event became more than just a race. It was a party.

Marguerite Mareuse

Men dominated the young sport of sports car racing. But women weren't left out. The first woman to drive in the Le Mans 24 was Marguerite Mareuse, in 1930.

A group of race fans enjoys a picnic during a race at the Brooklands racetrack in Weybridge, England.

The action on the track was simply the main attraction.

The Le Mans 24 led the way, but it wasn't the only sports car race. Other 24-hour races, such as the Brooklands Double 12, competed with the Le Mans. Shorter, more traditional Grand Prix races showed off raw speed. Longer races, such as the Mille Miglia (thousand miles) and the Targa Florio

The Brooklands racetrack was opened in 1907. The 2.75-mile (4.4 km) track was the first custom-built banked (slope-sided) raceway. The banking was nearly 30 feet (9 meters) high in places.

A car drives past spectators in Italy during the Mille Miglia in 1949.

(Florio plate or plaque) were the ultimate tests of endurance. The Targa Florio, for example, covered 277 miles (446 km) of Italian roads. It featured daunting mountain climbs, hairpin turns, and more.

In the 1930s and 1940s, sports car racing was also starting to catch on in the United States, but only at an amateur level. Other motor sports grabbed most of the U.S. headlines. The popular American sports included open-wheel car racing, stock car racing, and drag racing. Sports car racing was more like a hobby for Americans, and the races were not as competitive.

Mechanics inspect a damaged Ferrari during a race in Belgium in 1949. Ferraris took the sports car racing world by storm after World War II.

Decline and Rebirth

By the mid-1930s, world events were impacting the new sport. A workers' strike in France forced the 1936 Le Mans 24 to be canceled. Then, during World War II (1939–1945), Germany invaded France. The war ravaged France and turned people's attention to more serious matters. The race was canceled from 1940 until 1948. But racing didn't disappear completely.

A few minor races took place around France and other European countries. But the big one, the Le Mans 24, was on hold.

By 1949, life in France was getting back to normal. The Le Mans 24 was a symbol of national pride, and fans were excited to see the race start again. Cars had changed a lot over the years. Automakers knew that winning the Le Mans 24 would be a huge boost to sales. The Ferraris, Jaguars, and other models that raced over the next several years were truly built for speed. They had sleeker shapes and bigger engines with lots of horsepower. These changes made them faster than anything before. There was big money in the race for both drivers and automakers. Automakers sent several teams to the race, in hopes of increasing their chances to win.

Meanwhile, the sport was organizing. The World Sportscar Championship started in 1953 as a means of crowning a sports car racing champion. The races in the championship included many of the biggest races at the time.

British drivers Duncan Hamilton (at the wheel) and Tony Rolt (in glasses) with their winning Jaguar sports car after the 1953 Le Mans 24 Hours

Pierre Levegh *(above)* raced Formula 1 and sports cars from 1950 until his death in 1955. *Right:* Levegh is pictured in his Mercedes before the 1955 Le Mans.

The championship further ramped up the level of competition. The cars were getting faster and faster, and the number of entries was on the rise. Car manufacturers were entering the latest prototype cars. These cars were built specially for racing, but they were largely untested in real-world conditions.

All of this improvement came at a price—safety. Bigger and faster also meant more dangerous, as the racing world was soon to discover.

Tragedy

Sports car racing changed forever in 1955. Fans expected the Le Mans 24 that year to be a great race. Entries from Jaguar and Ferrari were favored to win.

Everything started out normally. But two and a half hours into the race, tragedy struck. Pierre Levegh was driving his Mercedes at full speed toward the pit area (where teams could work on their cars). Another driver pulled out of the pit in front of him. Levegh's car slammed violently into the other car. The Mercedes was launched into the air. It smashed into the barriers in front of the stands filled with fans, killing Levegh instantly.

The car's engine, transmission, and other parts burst into flames as they

Police race to the fiery scene of Levegh's accident during the 1955 Le Mans 24.

Volunteers and police help victims of Levegh's accident. It was the worst disaster in sports car racing history.

flew toward the stands. Spectators had no time to get out of the way. More than 80 fans were killed in the terrible accident, which made worldwide headlines. It was racing's darkest day.

The accident led the sport to start taking safety more seriously. Some races were canceled. Switzerland banned all circuit racing. Le Mans officials added concrete walls to prevent similar disasters. And Mercedes bowed out of auto racing altogether.

Despite the tragedy, the Le Mans 24 was back in 1956. But sports car racing would never be the same.

Growth in the United States

Europe remained the unofficial capital of sports car racing. But the sport was growing in the United States as well. For years, the Sports Car Club of America (SCCA) had organized sports car racing for amateurs. However, the SCCA was against professional races. The club saw the sport as a gentlemanly pastime. It didn't want racing to become a spending contest as it had in Europe. So racers competed for trophies, not money.

By 1958 drivers were demanding a chance to earn a living for what they did. Top sports car drivers turned to the United States Auto Club (USAC) for help. The USAC regulated popular open-wheel car racing. The drivers

The Most Dangerous Race

The Carrera Panamericana was a five-day race across Mexico. It started in 1950. The Mexican government organized the race to attract businesses to the country. But the race was widely believed to be the most dangerous in the world. Rough roads and wild country were only part of the problem. (In 1952 a vulture actually collided with the windshield of the winner's car.) Early on, many of the drivers were just regular Mexican citizens who wanted to get in on the action. Only about one-third of the entrants even finished the race. In five years of racing, 27 people were killed. After the 1955 disaster at Le Mans, the Mexican government decided the race was too dangerous and canceled future races. The race was revived in 1988 under better-regulated conditions.

U.S. drivers Marshall Teague *(left)* and Les Snow *(right)* attend to their Hudson Hornet during the 1952 Carrera Panamericana.

A Ferrari 250 GTO at the
Le Mans 24 Hours in 1963

urged the USAC to organize sports car races as well. And so the USAC Road Race Championship began in 1958. Dan Gurney, driving a Ferrari, became its first champion.

The SCCA's popularity took a huge hit. The group had no choice but to follow suit. By 1963, the SCCA's United States Road Racing Championship (USRRC) had replaced the USAC event.

The early 1960s were a golden age for sports car racing fans. New cars like the Ferrari GTO and the Corvette dominated races. The U.S. Grand Prix was a popular race held at Riverside, California, and later at Watkins Glen, New York. Sports car racing still didn't have the popularity of open-wheel car racing or stock car racing. But it was on the rise.

U.S. interest in the Le Mans 24 was also climbing. The Ford Motor Company, a U.S. automaker, badly wanted to win the race. The company even tried to buy the successful auto-maker Ferrari to achieve that goal. But the sale fell through. So Ford built its own car for the Le Mans. The result, the Ford GT40, dominated the Le Mans in the late 1960s. It became part of one of the great rivalries—Ford vs. Ferrari—in motor sports history.

Dan Gurney and A. J. Foyt's Ford Mark IV beats Chris Amon and Nino Vaccarella's Ferrari 330 P4 during the 1967 Le Mans 24.

The Ford GT40

Automaker Henry Ford II was determined to win the Le Mans 24. To do so, his Ford Motor Company partnered with a small company called Lola Cars International in the early 1960s. Lola had built the successful Lola GT. The partnership gave birth to a new sports car, the Ford GT40. (The GT in GT40 stands for Grand Touring and the 40 stands for 40 inches [100 centimeters], the height of the car.)

The new car first appeared at the Le Mans in 1964. It was a failure. None of the three Fords entered even finished the race. The 1965 race didn't go much better. But the company didn't give up. It brought an improved version to the 1966 race. There, the driving team of Bruce McLaren and Chris Amon finally gave Henry Ford his wish—a Le Mans victory. The win set off an era of Ford dominance. The GT40 went on to win the Le Mans in 1967, 1968, and 1969.

The winning team of Jacky Ickx and Jackie Oliver drove a Ford GT40 during the 1969 Le Mans 24.

Phil Hill *(left, number 15)*, driving a Chaparral prototype car, and A. J. Foyt *(right)*, in a Ford Mark II, lead the competition during the start of the Daytona 24 Hours.

Back in the United States, the Daytona 24 Hours was getting its start. This race was inspired by the Le Mans, but it was much different. The Daytona race was held at Daytona International Speedway. This closed oval course was nothing like the road racing at Le Mans.

Daytona's first 24-hour race was held in 1966. It quickly became another battleground for the Ford-Ferrari battle. After Ford took first place in the 1966 race, Ferrari stormed back in 1967 to claim the top three places. Ferrari even renamed one of its cars the Ferrari Daytona to honor the achievement. The rivalry increased the popularity of the sport in the United States. Sports car racing was reaching levels of popularity that it had never seen in North America.

Branching Out

By the late 1960s and 1970s, the sports cars used in racing were highly specialized. Grand Touring (GT) cars were based on the design of regular sports cars that anyone could buy at a dealership. The newest prototypes were unique, ultrapowerful racing machines. Ferrari, Lotus, Ford, and other builders competed fiercely with one another.

In the United States and Canada, this competition led to a new type of sports car race. Can-Am races featured only sports car prototypes competing in short, intense races. Having a winning car was a type of advertising that manufacturers just couldn't buy. So they spared no expense in building these racing machines.

A Ford prototype, 1967

A Porche 935K3 during the Le Mans 24 in 1980

New series that featured GT cars as well as prototypes were springing up everywhere. A series of races called the Le Mans Series started in Europe. The International Motor Sports Association (IMSA) GT Championship gained popularity in the United States. And the sport was also growing in Japan. The Super GT series and the Japan Le Mans Challenge were developed there.

But the sports car racing boom would not last in the United States. The Can-Am series died in 1974. It ended because of the high cost of operating a team and a decline in interest. The rise of stock car racing and the popularity of open-wheel car racing left sports car racing as an afterthought in U.S. motor sports.

The Porsche Years

Huge, gas-guzzling cars were popular in the early and mid-1970s. But fuel shortages during that decade forced automakers to rethink car design. Fuel efficiency became a must. Automakers made cars smaller so they would use less fuel. This trend found its way onto the racetrack as well. For a time, the Le Mans 24 even featured a special class—Group C—that focused on fuel efficiency.

Porsche dominated the Le Mans in the late 1970s and 1980s. It won every race from 1981 to 1987. Even more impressive, from 1982 to 1986, Porsche claimed the top six spots in every race! The level of competition evened out in the 1990s. But Porsche remained a threat to win every year.

American Resurgence

By the early 1990s, top-level sports car racing in the United States had all but disappeared. But late in the decade, the sport started to come back. The American Le Mans Series began in 1999. It had classes for both proto-types and GT cars. The series had both short sprint races and endurance races in the tradition of Le Mans. Other series—including the Grand-Am Series (which would in 2002 be renamed the Grand-Am Rolex Sports Car Series)—have helped to increase popularity in the United States.

The beginning of the twenty-first century was a good time to be a sports car racing fan. The sport was as popu-lar as ever in Europe. And it was finally making a comeback in the United States.

Cars roar around the Daytona International Speedway before day-break during the 2008 Rolex 24 Hour Race in Daytona, Florida.

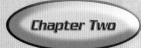

Chapter Two

Sports Car Racing Culture

Sports car racing is packed with speed, excitement, and danger. Drivers and their teams can compete in a variety of series. Most series have championships for individual race teams as well as manufacturer titles. Some series are focused in North America. Others have a more international flavor. The racing varies widely, from short sprints to grueling endurance races. But they have one thing in common. The cars are always the center of attention.

Racing Circuits

Europe has always been the center of the sports car racing world. Drivers and teams there can choose from a variety of racing series. The Le Mans

Series (LMS) is among the most popular. This series began as the Le Mans Endurance Series and focuses on long races. The Le Mans 24 is its biggest event. It includes four classes of cars—two GT classes and two prototype classes.

European teams aren't limited to just the LMS, though. The FIA GT3 European Championship and the World Touring Car Championship are series based on shorter races. And some countries, such as Great Britain and Germany, have their own series.

A pit crew races to make adjustments to the Audi driven by Germany's Marco Werner during the 2006 Le Mans 24.

The Le Mans Circuit

The course for the Le Mans 24 is called the Circuit de la Sarthe, after the French province where it is located. The most famous course in sports car racing has gone through a lot of changes over the years. In its original layout in 1923, it was 10.7 miles (17.2 km) long. Since the 1980s, it has been about 8.5 miles (13.7 km) long. It covers both public roads and sections especially built for racing. Throughout its history, some of the circuit's features have earned their own names. Here's the modern setup of the Le Mans circuit, along with some of those features.

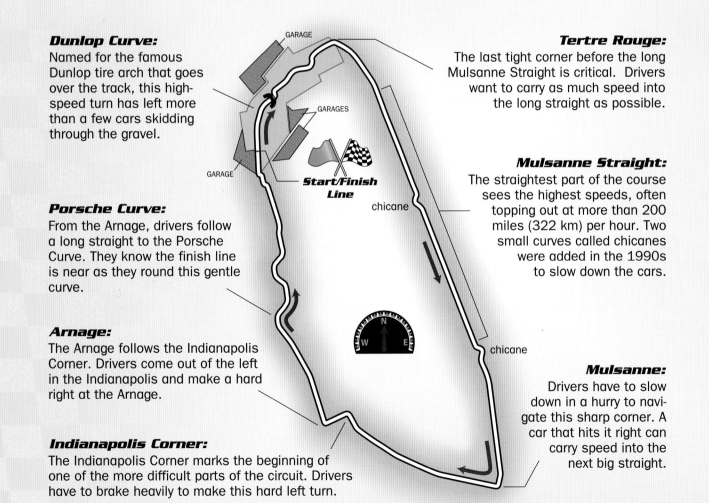

Dunlop Curve:
Named for the famous Dunlop tire arch that goes over the track, this high-speed turn has left more than a few cars skidding through the gravel.

Porsche Curve:
From the Arnage, drivers follow a long straight to the Porsche Curve. They know the finish line is near as they round this gentle curve.

Arnage:
The Arnage follows the Indianapolis Corner. Drivers come out of the left in the Indianapolis and make a hard right at the Arnage.

Indianapolis Corner:
The Indianapolis Corner marks the beginning of one of the more difficult parts of the circuit. Drivers have to brake heavily to make this hard left turn.

GARAGE

GARAGES

GARAGE

Start/Finish Line

chicane

chicane

Tertre Rouge:
The last tight corner before the long Mulsanne Straight is critical. Drivers want to carry as much speed into the long straight as possible.

Mulsanne Straight:
The straightest part of the course sees the highest speeds, often topping out at more than 200 miles (322 km) per hour. Two small curves called chicanes were added in the 1990s to slow down the cars.

Mulsanne:
Drivers have to slow down in a hurry to navigate this sharp corner. A car that hits it right can carry speed into the next big straight.

Sports car racing is more popular than ever in North America, although it still can't compare with stock car and open-wheel car racing. Fans and drivers have plenty of options. The American Le Mans Series (ALMS) leads the way. It is based on the European Le Mans Series, following the same basic rules and setup. The ALMS includes long endurance races and short sprints. Some races last 12 hours, while others take less than two hours.

The ALMS *(above right)* **has gained in popularity in the United States, although open-wheel car racing** *(top left)* **and stock car racing** *(bottom left)* **still dominate the U.S racing scene.**

Daytona Prototypes make their way to the start of the 2008 Rolex 24 in Daytona, Florida.

The Rolex Sports Car Series is another major championship based in North America. Formerly known as the Grand-Am series, it is built around the popular 24 Hours of Daytona race (also known as the Rolex 24). The series features both GT classes and prototypes. In 2003 the series debuted its own new class—Daytona Prototypes (prototypes built just for the series).

The series has drawn many of the top names in motor sports since it began in 1999. Stars such as Christian Fittipaldi, Juan Pablo Montoya, and Jeff Gordon gave the series instant credibility. The 24 Hours of Daytona is by far the series' biggest race. It draws thousands of U.S. fans, as well as flocks of Europeans who travel to Florida mainly to see the race.

The SCCA sanctions the SPEED World Challenge. The series is named for television's SPEED channel, which broadcasts the races. The series includes GT cars as well as a touring

2008 Rolex 24

A star-studded team of *(from left to right)* Juan Pablo Montoya, Dario Franchitti, Scott Pruett, and Memo Rojas won the 2008 Rolex 24 at Daytona. Their Lexus-powered Riley sports car won the race by about 7 miles (11 km).

car series. Touring cars are more limited in power and engine size, and they must be built to seat at least four people.

The Cars

For drivers and fans alike, the cars are what make sports car racing so exciting. There's something thrilling about watching a finely tuned Porsche or Ferrari hug the pavement as it takes a turn at top speed.

In racing, sports cars are split into two main groups: GT and prototypes. GT cars are based on popular sports cars such as Porsches and Ferraris. They have the same basic shape and style as production cars available to

1969 Pontiac Firebird Trans Am

Trans-Am

The Trans-American Sedan Championship (Trans-Am Series) was a popular sports car series that started in 1966. U.S. drivers and American-made cars such as the Corvette and the Mustang dominated the series. It became famous for its muscle cars of the 1970s. The Pontiac Trans Am was even named after it. But the popularity of the series faded over time. It stopped running after the 2005 season.

the public. But they're built just for racing, not for driving on regular roads.

Many series, including the Le Mans Series and the American Le Mans Series, further split GT cars into classes. GT1 includes the heaviest, most powerful cars. GT2 cars are a bit lighter. Some series feature GT3 cars, which are lighter still (and less expensive to build and maintain). In Japan, GT cars have more modifications and

are divided into GT500 and GT300 classes.

Prototypes (also known as Le Mans Prototypes or Daytona Prototypes) are specially built racing cars that aren't really based on production sports cars. Many of them are limited editions or one-offs. This means they're one of a kind. They're big, powerful, fast, and expensive. Like GT cars, prototypes are divided into classes based on weight. LMP1 and LMP2 are the

most common classes. The LMP1 class features the heaviest, fastest machines in sports car racing. They weigh more than 2,000 pounds (900 kilograms) and have huge engines.

At the Race

In any series, race day is the highlight of an event. But it takes a lot of work just to get to race day. Engineering teams spend years planning and

Right: **Fans photograph sports cars before the running of the 2006 Le Mans 24.** *Below:* **Drivers sign autographs for fans before race day.**

building their cars. Then drivers and race teams test them, tune them, and get them ready for the race.

Teams arrive at a track days before the race. They run practice laps and qualifying runs (shorter, timed runs to determine which drivers make it into the race). During qualifying, fans turn out to watch the cars race around the track one at a time. The driver with the fastest time gets to start at the front of the field, or the pole.

In the days leading up to a race, fans often have a chance to see their favorite cars and drivers up close. At most

races, fans have access to the garage area. They can take photos of cars, talk to team members, and get autographs. Keeping a relationship with the fans is something that almost everyone in the sport considers important.

On race day, fans flock to the track. Many dress in the colors of their favorite team or manufacturer. Most tracks have a large grandstand area with seats, vendors, and concessions (food and drinks). Large tracks with lots of twists and turns may have more than one set of stands. Fans get something to eat and find their way to their seats for the start of the race. For endurance races, which can last 12 hours or more, fans come and go throughout the race. But everyone is sure to be there for the finish.

Drivers and their teams make last-minute adjustments. Then it's time to hit the track. Excitement is high by the

Fans cheer as two Pescarolo-Judd prototypes cross the start/finish line at the 2005 Le Mans 24.

time the green flag starts the race. The roar of the engines fills the air as the racing begins.

Pit stops are among the most exciting parts of a race. In short races, speed is critical. Pit stops are usually very short, measured in seconds.

Teams add fuel and may change the tires. In endurance races, however, pit stops can last much longer. Teams may replace entire systems on the car, such as the brakes. A car can be in the pit for 30 minutes or more. And in endurance races, each car may have two or three

A pit crew rushes to change the tires and add fuel to this 2008 Pontiac/ Riley Daytona Prototype car during a pit stop at the 2008 Rolex 24.

drivers. The drivers take turns so they can stay fresh over such a long race.

The action on the track is fierce as the cars approach the checkered flag, which signals the end of the race. Drivers follow closely behind other cars in a strategy called drafting. Drafting reduces the amount of air resistance on the front of their cars. With less resistance, they can go a few miles per hour faster.

Drivers steer their cars deep into turns, waiting as long as possible to brake. They battle for every position. In the end, one car wins. The driver heads to the victory circle to celebrate with the team and the fans. Then the teams pack up the cars and get ready to do it all over again at the next race.

Being the first to come under the checkered flag for the win is the ultimate goal for every race team. Here, drivers Nick Ham and David Haskell celebrate their victory at the 2008 Rolex 24.

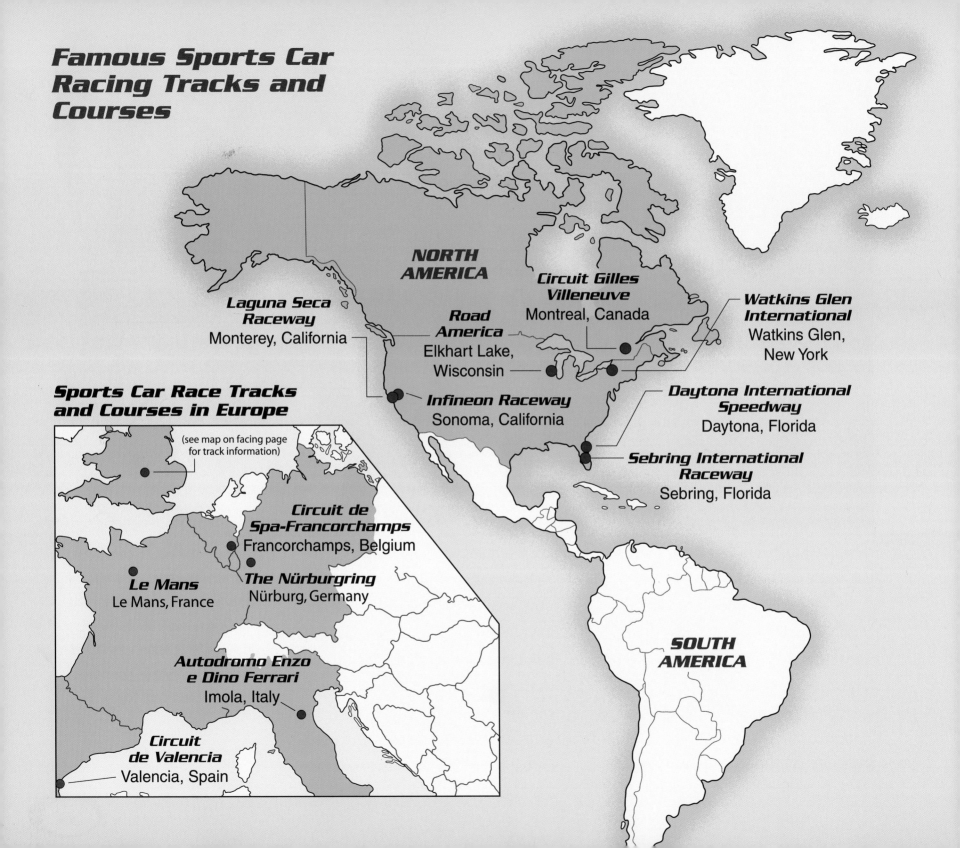

Famous Sports Car Racing Tracks and Courses

NORTH AMERICA

Laguna Seca Raceway
Monterey, California

Road America
Elkhart Lake, Wisconsin

Circuit Gilles Villeneuve
Montreal, Canada

Infineon Raceway
Sonoma, California

Watkins Glen International
Watkins Glen, New York

Daytona International Speedway
Daytona, Florida

Sebring International Raceway
Sebring, Florida

SOUTH AMERICA

Sports Car Race Tracks and Courses in Europe

(see map on facing page for track information)

Circuit de Spa-Francorchamps
Francorchamps, Belgium

Le Mans
Le Mans, France

The Nürburgring
Nürburg, Germany

Autodromo Enzo e Dino Ferrari
Imola, Italy

Circuit de Valencia
Valencia, Spain

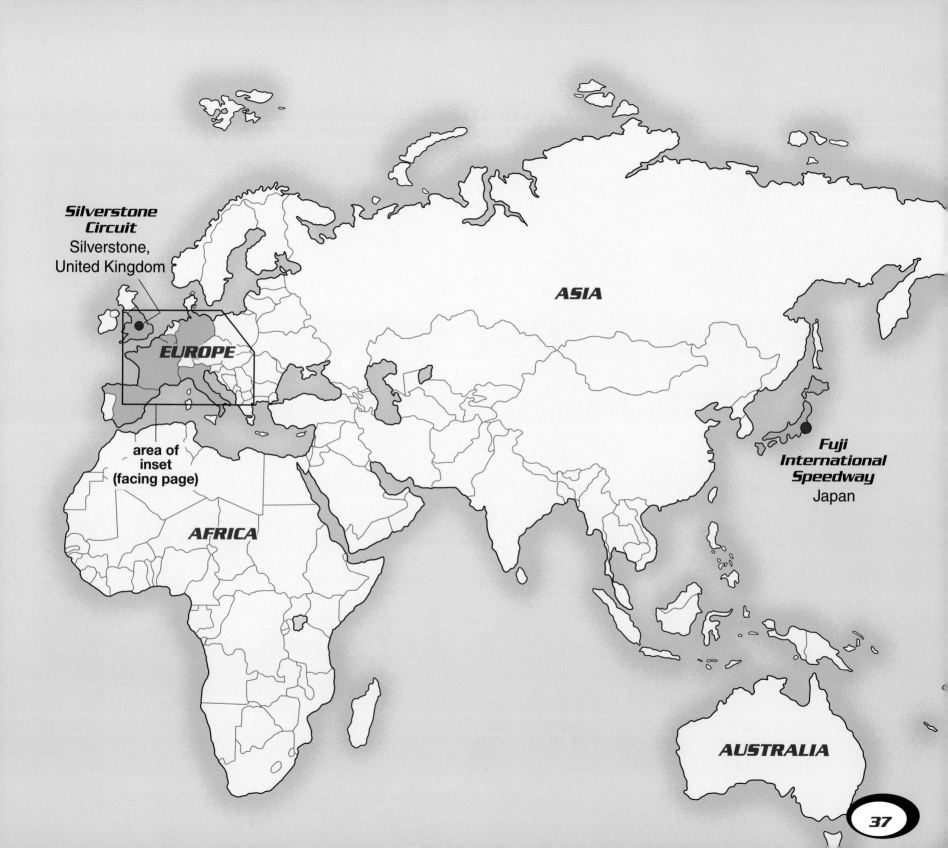

Silverstone Circuit
Silverstone,
United Kingdom

area of
inset
(facing page)

EUROPE

ASIA

AFRICA

Fuji International Speedway
Japan

AUSTRALIA

Audi R8

The greatest prototype of the twenty-first century so far has been the Audi R8. After claiming third and fourth places in 1999, the 3.6-liter (1 gallon), twin-turbocharged R8 raced to the top three spots in 2000. The R8 won again in 2001, 2002, 2004, and 2005 before giving way to the Audi R10 in 2006.

Audi R10

Audi's diesel-powered R10 took the design of the world's best sports car—the R8—and improved on it. The R10 dominated from the moment Audi introduced it. It won its first race, the 12 Hours of Sebring, Florida, in March 2006. And it hasn't lost at Le Mans, winning in 2006, 2007, and 2008.

Daytona Prototype

Daytona Prototypes are the Rolex Sports Car Series' answer to the powerful Le Mans Prototypes. Like the Le Mans Prototypes, they're built just for racing. But they're also built to be a bit slower and less expensive. The idea is that they can compete at a high level but not be merely a test of which automaker is willing to spend the most money to build one.

Porsche 911

The Porsche 911 is probably the most famous sports car in racing. Designed in 1963, it has been in continuous production since the mid-1960s and has won more races than any other car. Pictured here is a Porsche 911 GT3 in the Petit Le Mans (part of the American Le Mans Series) at Road Atlanta in October 2008.

Shelby Cobra 427

The sleek Shelby Cobra was proof that sports car racing didn't end with Le Mans in the 1960s. The 427's V8 engine didn't stack up at sports car racing's most famous track, but it was a force in the FIA World Manufacturer's Championship, winning it in 1965.

Ferrari 375 Plus

Ferrari emerged as a sports car racing power with its first Le Mans 24 victory in 1954. The 375 Plus lacked the aerodynamic grace of many of its competitors. But its huge V12 engine more than made up for that with sheer horsepower.

Alfa Romeo 8C

In the early 1930s, the Alfa Romeo 8C was all but unbeatable. Their supercharged, 2.3-liter (0.6 gallon) engines powered them to four straight Le Mans wins, from 1931 to 1935. The Alfa Romeo's greatest success came in 1933, when the 8C finished in the top three spots.

Aston Martin DBR1

British automaker Aston Martin claimed its first—and only—Le Mans win in 1959 with the DBR1. Drivers Roy Salvadori and Carroll Shelby won the race when the more powerful Ferraris suffered from overheating problems. The DBR1's 2.6-liter (0.7 gallon) engine also powered it to success in the World Sportscar Championship.

Ferrari 275P

Ferrari's dominance in the early 1960s was so complete that the Ford Motor Company tried to buy the small Italian automaker. The Ferrari 275P was one in a line of Ferrari winners. The mid-engine, 3.3-liter (0.9 gallon) 275P raced to the 1964 Le Mans victory, edging out two more powerful Ferrari 330Ps.

Ford GT40

The GT40 was the result of Henry Ford II's obsession with winning Le Mans. Ford unseated Ferrari as the dominant car of the day with the GT40, which featured a small block engine and took inspiration from successful open-wheel cars. The GT40 helped give Ford four straight wins from 1966 to 1969.

Porsche 956

The rise of Porsche began in the 1970s with the 936. By the early 1980s, the improved Porsche 956 prototype was dominating courses around the world. With its lightweight aluminum cockpit and its turbocharged 6.25-liter (1.6 gallon) engine, the 956 was a beast on the track. It won Le Mans every year from 1982 through 1985.

Bentley Sport

In the 1920s, the Bentley was the car to beat at the Le Mans. The Sport won the second Le Mans race in 1924 with an average speed of 53.8 miles (86.6 km) per hour. Then it won again in 1927 before giving way to newer models.

Dodge Viper GTS-R

With 500 horsepower and an aluminum V10 engine, the Dodge Viper GTS-R dominated GT sports car racing in 2000, when it took the Rolex 24 as well as the Le Mans 24 GT2 class. Legendary automobile designer Carroll Shelby helped develop the Viper, which first appeared in 1992.

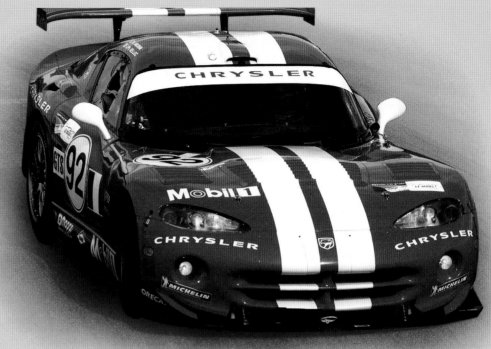

Bentley Speed 8

The Bentley company, which had not raced in 73 years, returned to racing in 2001 with the Bentley EXP Speed 8, a Le Mans Prototype. EXP Speed 8s took third place at the Le Mans 24 in 2001 and fourth place in 2002. In 2003, with a 3.6-liter (1 gallon) V8 race engine—and called simply the Speed 8—Bentley finally won the Le Mans 24.

Matra-Simca MS670 Prototype

Matra-Sports, a French company, was founded in 1964 and became an endurance racing powerhouse during the late 1960s and early 1970s. This MS670 prototype, powered by a monstrous V12 engine, won the 1972 Le Mans 24 by traveling 2,915.1 miles (4,691 km) at an average speed of 121.45 mph (195.45 km/hour).

Mazda 787B

The 787B is the only Japanese-made car ever to win the Le Mans 24. Its 1991 victory was quite a shock to Mercedes and Jaguar, the two heavy favorites in the race. While Mazda lacked the power of these heavyweights, it was more reliable and fuel efficent. The black periscope-style air intakes just inside the rear fenders could be raised or lowered depending on car and racing conditions.

Glossary

aerodynamic: shaped to cut through the air with little resistance

chicane: a tight turn or series of tight turns in an otherwise straight stretch of track

circuit: a racetrack or racecourse

drafting: following closely behind another car in order to reduce air resistance and increase speed

endurance: the ability to perform a task for a long period of time

grand touring (GT): a type of sports car closely related to mass-production sports cars. GT racing cars are specially built, but they look like the road cars they're modeled after.

horsepower: a measure of an engine's power

performance: a car's speed and handling

pole: the first starting spot for a race

prototype: a test car or a car not built for mass production. In sports car racing, prototypes are the fastest, most expensive cars.

qualifying: the timed laps each car runs alone on a circuit before a race. The starting grid is determined by qualifying times.

starting grid: the order in which cars begin a race

Selected Bibliography

Friedman, Dave. *Modern GT Racing: Today's Fastest Cars on the World's Greatest Tracks*. St. Paul, MN: Motorbooks, 2007.

———. *Pro Sports Car Racing in America, 1958–1974*. Osceola, WI: Motorbooks, 1999.

Laban, Brian. *Le Mans 24 Hours*. St. Paul, MN: MBI Publishing Company, 2001.

Lynch, Michael T., William Edgar, and Ron Parravano. *American Sports Car Racing in the 1950s*. Osceola, WI: Motorbooks, 1999.

Further Reading

Donovan, Sandy. *Sports Cars*. Minneapolis: Lerner Publications Company, 2007.

Fox, Martha Capwell. *Car Racing*. San Diego: Lucent Books, 2004.

Oxlade, Chris. *Sports Cars*. Chicago: Raintree, 2005.

Schleifer, Jay. *Le Mans!: Race around the Clock*. Parsippany, NJ: Crestwood House, 1995.

Websites

American Le Mans Series
http://www.americanlemans.com
This page has all the latest news and results from this popular sports car racing series. Photos, race highlights, schedules, and more make it a must-see for fans of the series.

ESPN—Racing
http://sports.espn.go.com/rpm/racing/index
ESPN's racing center includes news, features, and results from all sorts of motor sports, from NASCAR to motorcycle racing to sports car racing.

Grand-Am
http://www.grand-am.com
Visit this page to learn all about the Rolex Sports Car Series including the 24 Hours of Daytona. It includes schedules, results, team news, and plenty of photographs.

24 Hours of Le Mans
http://www.lemans.org/accueil/index_gb.html
The English-language version of the official website of the Le Mans 24 includes information about the race and the course, as well as information for visitors.

Index

About the Author

Matt Doeden is a freelance author and editor and an avid car racing fan. He has written more than forty books, including several on stock car racing and its drivers. He has also edited hundreds of books for kids on a wide range of subjects.

About the Consultant

Jan Lahtonen is a safety engineer and auto mechanic. He has raced sports cars and worked as a performance driving instructor. He has followed car racing for more than 40 years.

Photo Acknowledgments

The images in this book are used with the permission of: © Brian Cleary/Getty Images for Grand Am, pp. 4–5, 24–25; © National Motor Museum/HIP/The Image Works, pp. 6, 7, 40 (top), 41 (both), 43 (top); AP Photo, pp. 6–7 (background), 10 (background), 12, 14 (left), 17; © Fox Photos/Hulton Archive/Getty Images, pp. 8, 43 (bottom); © Topical Press Agency/Hulton Archive/Getty Images, p. 9; © ANSA/CORBIS, p. 11; © Ronald Startup/Picture Post/Getty Images, pp. 13, 40 (bottom); © Bert Hardy/Picture Post/Getty Images, p. 14 (right); © Empics/Alpha/SportsChrome, pp. 15, 16; © Klemantaski Collection/Hulton Archive/Getty Images, pp. 18 (top), 22; © DPPI/Icon SMI, p. 18 (bottom); © Schlegelmilch/CORBIS, pp. 19, 45 (top): © Bettmann/CORBIS, pp. 20, 21; AP Photo/Darryl Graham, p. 23; © Bryn Lennon/Getty Images, p. 25; © Gavin Lawrence/Getty Images, pp. 27 (top left), 31 (top); AP Photo/Carolyn Kaster, p. 27 (bottom left); AP Photo/Steve C. Wilson, p. 27 (right); AP Photo/David Graham, p. 28; AP Photo/Terry Renna, p. 29; © Jerry Heasley, p. 30; © Darrell Ingham/Getty Images, p. 31 (bottom); © Denis Lambert/Maxppp/ZUMA Press, p. 32 (top); © Herve Petitbon/Maxppp/ZUMA Press, p. 32 (bottom); © ALAIN JOCARD/AFP/Getty Images, p. 33; REUTERS/Dave Ferrell, pp. 34, 35; © Sutton Motorsports/ZUMA Press, pp. 38 (top), 44 (bottom), 45 (bottom); © V. Michel/Fep/Panoramic/ZUMA Press, p. 38 (bottom); AP Photo/David Pitt, p. 39 (top); © Streeter Lecka/Getty Images, p. 39 (bottom); © Roger-Viollet/The Image Works, p. 42 (both); © Matt Turner/ALLSPORT/Getty Images, p. 44 (top). Illustrations by © Laura Westlund/Independent Picture Service.

Cover: © Gavin Lawrence/Getty Images.